BUTTERFLY TATTOO

By
Paul Johan Stokstad

BLUE LIGHT PRESS • 1ST WORLD LIBRARY

1ST WORLD
PUBLISHING

SAN FRANCISCO • FAIRFIELD • DELHI

BUTTERFLY TATTOO
Copyright ©2012 by Paul Johan Stokstad

For information contact:

1ST WORLD PUBLISHING
809 S. 2nd Street
Fairfield, IA 52556
www.1stworldpublishing.com

BLUE LIGHT PRESS
www.bluelightpress.com
Email: bluelightpress@aol.com

COVER AND BOOK DESIGN:
Melanie Gendron

AUTHOR WEBSITE:
www.stokstad.com

FIRST EDITION

LCCN: 2012911340

ISBN 9781421886466

ACKNOWLEDGEMENTS

I'd like to thank the following anthologies in which some of these poems appeared:

Collecting Moon Coins,
Collecting Moon Coins Volume II,
This Enduring Gift

I'd like to thank Corinne Erly and Clouds de Narvaez for their intrepid typing support.

Let us all praise Diane Frank for inspiring many and publishing all of these poems.

DEDICATION

This book is dedicated to Ruth Eleanor Feggestad Stokstad, who taught me to be still, observe, love, and then write about it.

CONTENTS

love

The Picture of You

The sun is on the screen
behind your shoulder

This pastel blouse
striped red, blue

That little arm, barely
visible

And, mouth parted slightly
there's a subtle shade of
pink on your cheek

You may not believe in God
but, you are everything divine
to me.

You're the Most

You're the most
beautiful thing I've ever seen,
which is saying a lot

because I've seen
a single rose
in a silver vase

the sun
illuminating the underside
of fifty clouds

two chickadees
pecking for dinner, alone
outside a lecture hall

and a flower petal
purple, against a
white sink

Tonight, for Dawn

Silent Silver River

Flowing like
A Chinese Milky Way
Forever
From my dark room
To your raucous laughter.

She is also sweet,
It is also sweet, this laugh,
And your face shines up
Like the only girl
I've seen in months

And your dance
Like the May-Princess,
Clear-eyed, tells,

That the question you are
Only first love will answer
With something like that

Silent Silver River

Bright Lotus, You are

Bright Lotus, you are
Married to a foreign prince
Living in a southern land
Where snow no longer touches you.

I am
Going through the autumns
Two thousand miles to the North.

Today, the carp swam
To the top of the quiet river

A bird
Dipped in flight
Almost touching
Our former meeting place

Yes, I still love you

But, I do not miss you
Since I am in love
With what you are

And nowadays,
I see you everywhere.

Love is My Religion

Yes, I confess
I lost touch with Jesus.
So long
I've been studying
In Diana's Temple
Think of what she's taught me:

The backs of hands
Left corners of mouths
A smooth, soft touch.

This that I'm preaching
Is true platonic love
Not alone or handless:

Learn to love
Learn to love you
Learn to love
Learn to love me
Learn to love
Learn to love God.

This is what happens
One Way or another.
This is the way
Back to love Jesus
Perfectly

It's The Most Beautiful

It's the most beautiful probably
Time of the year

The most lovely
Motion we could make
Is turning toward

Mountains and hills toss
Shadows like
Faces on each other

Not a thing, other
Than a girl I know
Playing tennis,
Naked to the waist

On the fence
In the sun, a cardinal
And now, I wonder

Holding you when
Air is
Warm with sighs

Starting to rain
Its grey out

Running on
Wet leaves
Like leather to me

Outside it snows
Things quiet down
I put the clock in the drawer

A Dream Just to Dream

In a magical dream just to dream
There was a lady
And a sudden shower
From somewhere, to which
She opened her blouse
To receive the rain
And myself, saying
"I'll keep you warm all night"

And that was Kay, I know
And also
There I was dancing
On widespread and various hills
In a leotard
So fast, and joyous

And far away from the warehouse
Of my daily life, and amazed

At the clarity of a dream.

Perry&Bart

I've made this
Imaginary child
Perry&Bart
With you
Via transcendental
Insemination.
We have this family
In thought.
You are one woman
I wanted to have children with
and now it's done
In the timeless world
Of immaculate
Conception.

In the White Dawn, at Breaking of the Day

I remember you there
Off in D.C.
And how beautiful you were
Even then.

Now, I imagine,
You are even more beautiful.

Title courtesy *Chanson de Roland*
Laisse 53, line 7.

I like you.

You keep listening
even when I'm not talking.

What's your mother's middle name?

Do you or do you not
like sour strawberry gum?

Probably the Better of the Two

A soft quiet hug
Your very blue shorts
And silent blanket

Deep in the starry night
Just outside
Of innocence

May I tell you
That the way you kiss
Met me like no other

Way of being held
Like only you
Could ever hold me

The Button

The room on the top floor
At 115 Fairchild
The east, south, and west sides windowed

Joni Mitchell singing
Sisowtowbell Lane

Constant Comment tea
Already slightly
Passé

You with your
Stormy head
Of dark brown hair
You with your layers
And layers
Of brown and white clothing

You and I,
Intensely discussing
Gershwin, Piaf, and Ibsen

You and I
Wrestling and
Laughing

And then me
Alone

As I undid
In deep gravity
The last button
On your blouse.

lost

Dream

This perfectly soft
And late
Evening in Iowa City

Snow falling
In perfect quiet

I'm sitting alone

Today

That lady's arm
Swinging, in their car
Over his shoulder

The sound of the
Summer tunes
On the paint spattered radio
From around the side corner
Of the house

The silver sheen to the
Leaves on the tree
Behind the house
Wistey and I
Were scraping down
When you drove up

Our marriage
Was dissolved
Four days ago

But I didn't know
Until you stopped by
With papers
Today.

Available Soon: Used Husband

One Owner.
Runs well (plays tennis).
Kisses like new.

Well Trained.
Dishwashing.
Replacing Toothpaste Cap.
Taking out the trash.

Mind in good condition.
Heart needs work.

Far Richer, Far Poorer

Patty your
Slow sad frown
Meaning you're thoughtful
Not sad,

Patty your
Slow sad frown
Is with me now.

How to Avoid Women

Wear Brown.

Do not go to bars, airports, or sewing circles
If you are in school, avoid majoring
In Elementary Ed, Library Science, French.
Study Linguistics, and argue for
The systematic phonemic level:
this gets you nowhere with women nowadays.

Carry an umbrella, unless it's raining.

Carrying a purse helps,
Unless you live in New York'
Where everyone carries a purse.

There are places you can go
Where you will rarely meet women:
The Greenland Ice Cap
Marine Corps barracks
Near billboards.

Become a monk.
If you are already a monk,
Take vows of silence.

Do all of the following:

Get plenty of rest

Eat three meals a day
Brush after meals, and floss at night
Bathe daily
Collect stamps or butterflies
The combination of the above listed items
Has the effect of filling your day up
Completely and you never run into women.

Wear brown.

If you are already wearing brown
Wear yellow socks.

If you play tennis, play at 6:30
(for some reason, women don't play at 6:30,
morning or evening)

Play singles.
Your doubles partner may have friends.

Finally, if none of these things work,
You may try the following, in combination:

Collect snakes
Spend a lot of time with your eyes closed

Wear brown.

Flower Rescue

Sometime back
We met behind Eicher's Florist
And, sorting out a few
Tired roses

To freshen up a bit
For a little while longer

Tired, I wish I could be
Picked out of this
Barrel to be freshened

By a little while longer
With you

Diann

Head resting against the curled

fingers of my hand,

hair on the side of my face

pushed upward,

I think of you.

I've placed my wedding ring
on the dryer.

It's hard to get it off.
Swollen fingers from the dishes.

I need a little
romance in my life.

I had a wife once

I had a wife once
She would stand by the closet and dress
Somewhere in Iowa City
Overlooking the campus
In married student housing

She was
Perfectly beautiful
A symmetry of nakedness

Two rooms
Two people
Two directions

Those days are gone
Forever, but
May she someday
find that happiness
She left me for

Do you

ever think

of me?

Throwing Away Your Hair

I threw away the Easter basket
full of your hair today.

Yes, the hair I had saved
off the salon floor
when you cut it in a tiff
after the play.

The hair that I first held in my hands
when I kissed you, in character, onstage
and also, out of character, in bed.

The hair that I had to hide
when we broke up
so as not to cry.

The hair that still has your smell on it
nine months later.

That hair.

I was thinking of taking it to the new bridge
over the Mississippi in Burlington
and walking it out to the middle
right here in December
and while people drive by
laughing and yelling "Don't jump"
dropping it, curl by curl
into the relentless brown water.

But no, I decided to let go of you two days ago

and today I got up and dumped the whole pile
into the trash can, basket and all.

It's over there right now.

I haven't bothered to take it out to the dumpster.
So other stuff is piling up on it, as it joins the mix
of discarded things, and someday soon
it'll go out and then I'll be done with it.

Now if I could just get your hair
off of my naked shoulder at night
like when I held you while you slept.

Now if I could just get your hair
off of my chest
while I meditate
since we did that,
leaning together,
holding each other close.

Now if I could just get your hair
out of my head.

For You

I'll see you in twelve years
In some gymnasium—turned ballroom
Piano playing

You'll be talking to an artist
And in a lag

I'll wander up & ask

"May I have this dance?"
and, unlike those around us,
improvising,

You'll remember and I'll remember
Perfect waltz.

I'll always love you.

and found

Want Ad

I want to run through the
Cedar Rapids airport
And catch Kathy Sloan
In a tight embrace
Her hair in a storm
And her 112-pound body
Layered and layered
In various shades of brown

Where is she now?

I'd like to knock on Diann's
bedroom window at 3 A.M.
and have her come out
in the backyard
with those cotton pyjamas
and a light blue blanket
and see that I love her
again.

I want Renee to be happy
And find the guy she's looking for
It must be that
He does exist.

I want various
Perfect lovers
To meet the tiny group
Of women
Who have let me kiss them
and like Krishna
meeting milkmaids
fulfill them.

I want to spend
More time
With you

Just to watch
You move
And smile
And to hold what there is
Of such a model
Woman

Safe from being alone
Whatsoever.

Like the Robin's Egg

Like the robin's egg
Waiting at the edge
Of being blue
And not being

Your skin approaches
The junction point
Of Being
And becoming

Like candy for the fingers

Touching you
I can never be sure
Whether I've touched
The truly real

Or it's just
That my fingertips
Are dreaming

Bubbles

Doyne's off to work
Swanson on the phone
& eating the oatmeal
you made

It's meditation
time, and it's great
having a woman's voice in the house

Peaslee

It's one o'clock

So

Where are you
Fast asleep tonight?

Or are you
Unfastened, alone
With the stars and space

All asleep in body
All awake in mind

Are you as silent in sleep
As you are in action?

Or are you talking
With angels
Or dreaming, something finding
Completion at last?

Who knows?
I always think of you
Seen from the left, passing

Finding You

For a long time
you were a
small, leaping wildebeest
crossing the road
in front of my
Toyota four wheeler
seen for a moment
and then
disappearing
into the jungle.

You were a
long Chinese kite
visible
ten miles away
from an ocean steamer
somewhere
in a section edited out
of a yellowed, 1930's
paperback
adventure novella.

You were
a tie-dyed
scarf
draped over a string
on sale
close to
Fisherman's Wharf.

You were
a heron's wing
beating and beating
as the bird
called
far off
for a mate.

But now, my
search for you
has narrowed down.

Now you are revealed
as a lot
less elusive
as a matter of fact.

The place that I found you in
was a small, strong place
a place of definition
and stability.
You did not waver
and appear exotic
or unusual.
You were there
just like a cello player
solid, lyrical, and present.

The place where I found you
was a clean place
with shape and
tone.
There was nothing extra there
or anything
unneeded.

The place where you are
it turns out
is a place where
few other people
have chosen to hide:
unmoving
unshaken
in plain sight
close at hand
right
in front of me

in the open.

Pamela

When I last saw you
You disappeared with a cry
Into the doorway
Of your curved dormitory

Like the inviolate entry
At the top of a Valentine
Heart

Like the open end
Of a mother's arms
Reaching to embrace

Like the French curve
From your waist to your hip
And the gentle, white valley
Down your chest.

Amherst

I offer to you
The forty thousand sparkles
On a snowy hill
Passed yesterday

You have had my
Secret thoughts
these days

And I can imagine
Leaving the group, somewhere
Say in Massachusetts

And walking the cool, dark
Oak and Maple avenues
of a college town

That would be memorable, with you
Your talk so bright
your kiss intoxicating.

(I can't get you out of my system
like an unfinished
synchrony)

Once we touched
but now must idealize
at a distance

So,
Until we meet again

All I have to give
is snow sparkle,
secret thoughts

and to let you know
I've been loving you.

Yesterday, the word

adorable

came up, and then

I thought of you.

Missy

I am in Love

with that
steely little mind
with that
sharply chiseled face

The Fantasy:

It's 6:30 A.M.
and a sunlit summer room
and waking up to you
all in white
sheets

and your sharply chiseled face
is softened by sleep,
but then, awaking
your steely blue eyes

open, and it's divine
to be lying with you and awakening.

And Yet:

It's someone else
lying with you and awakening
it is his morning
and he is your Love

Still, he is my representative
my congressman

he loves you for me
he loves you in case
I never see you again

He loves you and never knows
that through his eyes
I see you
and through his love
I Love you

(forgive me, for
I am in love

with that
steely little, blue-eyed mind
with that sharply-chiseled, sleepy face.)

California Dreamer

Long hair, perfect health, clear thinking
You bring
Like a California Girl
Filled with mountains and ocean and
Yosemite National Forest

You seem to be made
of pine air and climbing
Redwood studded slopes
Those red cheeks reddening
And those blue eyes bright

How can it be
That your room is so cold
With fresh air
And your bed is so warm
With love?

Dancing With You

I ask a question
Your answer says yes
But with arching roses
And curliqued sequins

I write a line
You reply
With sprays of violet
And tiny bells.

I put up a building,
You instantly add
Chandeliers, banners,
And stained glass windows.

I lift you straight up in the air
You turn it all
Into long, lyrical tails
Of Chineses kites,
Pink and blue lights,
And a little lace.

I am the writer
Making a statement,
You are the poet
Coming back
With nuance, frill,
Subtle but strong
Comment
And beauty,

And through it all
You move in shapes
Simply made
For staring adoration.

Frag/Haiku

It's always like this

the night air, steamy, and you,

possibility

Haiku Women

Missy:
I loved you too much
To explain. No way. Grass still
May be matted there.

Donna:
And now this burning
Love makes me better, and you
It just illumines

Katharine:
Your dark eye shadow
You loved the back of children's
Heads. Where are you now?

Your name was Paula
We had much in common. You
Moved away at six

How To Pick Up A Woman

In order to pick her up you
Bring her into your strength
That is
You bring her to you
Rather than leaning over
Or trying to go meet her
You have to bring her over
Right in front of you
and bend your knees
keeping your back straight
It's important
That you don't bend over
Because then you
Won't be strong
And you can hurt your back
So bend your knees and
Just pick her up
With your left arm
Around her left side
At the waist
And the right on her right leg
Just above the knee
But you don't really lift her
With your arms
Because they aren't
As strong as when you
Bend your knees
Get down
Bring her securely to your chest
With your arms

51

And then lift her into the air
By straightening your legs
Like lifting in the workplace
You use your legs
Not your back
The thing is to bring her into
Your place of strength
From where you can easily lift
and carry and move her
Around in a circle in the air
You don't need to go to her
Just guide her
To that place
Where you are the most comfortable
And the most powerful
And then you can uplift
And protect her
With ease.

I still
Fly with you
Darling
In the clear blue night sky
Of imagination

My Love

My love is at the tips
Of five tenderly moving fingers
as they barely touch the tiny hairs
And slightly warm the skin
At your waist, and, moving
Slowly up your side,
Around behind your back
And on up, getting lost
In the wisps at the back of your neck

My love is flowing out of my chest
In a way that I physically feel
Flowing into your chest

My love is the yellow flower
By the sunlit open window
Waiting for a breeze to take its scent
To you, dreaming, partly dressed,
Asleep, in white flannel sheets

My love is a space bigger than a boxcar
Full of air, bigger than a football stadium
Full of people, bigger than the space
You see when you lie on your back
In summer night Cedar Falls, Iowa
And stare straight up, watching for
Bright streaks against a dark blue.

Bigger than the biggest

And all of That big, deep, immoveable Space
Is now moving toward you
Due to arrive, sometime in the next
Very intent five minutes.

My love, calm, giving, playful, happy
My love, fixing things at your house,
My love, washing your dishes
So that you can have a rest

My love for myself
Now measuring women and relationships
Not by how they look or what we say
But by how I feel,
The chair in the room
I find myself in.

My love, now giving to me
as practice, and to open
an enormous space
for giving more to you
when you become
part of me.

My love, patient, enduring,
Waiting for your moment too.

My love, quiet, happy, full tonight.
You now sleeping about a mile away.

You said you are waiting
For doubtless love in my eyes
So that we can open up again
The deep stuff, that has already
Made us a legendary, historic
Power center of love.

My love, hear this,
My eyes are open, looking to you
With that doubtless love.

And my love
Remembering last month
When my love, and my loved
Left the walls of this, my room,
Permanently blushing.

Heart Country

There's a country
Within your country.
I know because
I travelled there last week.

It's an independent state
Filled with feeling, light, and blood.

In that country,
I never had to walk,
But was held, like a leaf
Floating in a pink, inland sea.

In that country
There is a little white flower
With roots so red
You can use them to color anything.

In that country
I was already a citizen

And we spoke
All the languages of the world
Over the slow thunder
Of a grand, beating heart.

Still Life

The sunset over the highway
The branches of the leafless grove
Simplified to a flat pattern of black lace

All the memories
Now that I am
Forty

Held in a single view

And now you,
Flying and then stopping
Branch to branch

Now I see you
Now I don't

With a
Sky pink
Behind a black lace
fabric

Dating Yourself

Why not
Date yourself
For a while

And change
Loneliness to solitude

Time to
Lie down
Close your eyes
And ask yourself
Where is this feeling
In my body

Where is this
Jealousy, insecurity
Uncertainty, sense of
Isolation, or even
Happiness
In my body

It's there, and you can find it
In your throat
In your heart
In your stomach

Be there, with it
Ask it what it is
what it's name is
When it first felt like this
In your body

Then ask
What it needs
And then
You go ahead
And give it to it

Your loneliness needs your attention
Your insecurity needs your commitment

Your happiness needs to be appreciated
And cultivated
By you first
Before anyone else
Can get the hint

Prime the pump.
Start showing the world
What you deserve
By giving it to yourself
And then the rest of us
Will do the same

You must create this
Loving space
Within and for
Yourself

So that
You become
Not only nice
To strangers

Because you have love
There

Inside you
Instead of inattention
And neglect.
Then the closer
People get to you
The more love they get

That's the list.
Gather information from your body
Become an expert on the truth
Of what you feel
Because your body
Tells you
Create a loving space
And then go out and date yourself
That is, look for you

The you that you want to be
The you that you really are
The you that is great
And happy and whole
And running smoothly
Like an ocean liner on a pleasure cruise

Look for yourself
Being yourself
When you are with someone
Look for someone
With whom you feel
You are being yourself

Not twisting, hopping, jumping, crawling,
Climbing, falling, needing, controlling
Grasping, pushing, begging, telling, losing

Or gaining
Just you being you
But with company

Analyze them by how much
You you are
Remember to feel love is
More than to feel loved

Get out there
And date yourself
I'm sure you'll
Find somebody
You like.

wisdom

Dancing with a Poet

What is it that twirls
When a poet twirls
When I curl you in
To a tight, tango-like
Formation, and stop.
And what is it that
Stops?

Is it your hair so black
Cut like an ancient
Egyptian?

Is it your eyes so big
That never seem to
blink?

Or is it a world that twirls
When a poet spins
Or another galaxy
Depending on the poet

Of unusual birds, lost
Expanses, obser-
vations, clarifi-
cations
and nuance?

Think of
What would happen
If a poet really turned
Whole planets

New and foreign
Or at least entire
Conceptual spaces
Spinning at the basis
Of everything

And then when I dip you sideways
In a dramatic fall
Then does all of life
Become horizontal
In some unknown way
While you see just
The ceiling overhead

And then what,
When I dare
To lift you, turning,
Up in the air
Like a slowly circling eagle

As if all that could be lifted
And all that could be turned

Yes,
I just can't say
What happens
Then, but
When I show you
One good turn
And then another

You turn, you flash
You exhibit grace
Life, spunk
and beauty

and yet somehow
when I turn
this Egyptian-looking
slender
black-eyed poet

I feel a kind of thrill
of standing
next to immortality
next to a source
and a soul
of literature

and I think
that maybe if I put
a little extra beauty
and a twist
of imagination
into our dance
that you of all people,
will understand it
that you of all people
will perceive it fully
and that our dance perhaps
will come out someday
in one of your poems
as a heron's wing,
a brief, enigmatic
point,
or a message
straight from the feeling level
to all creation

I guess it's just because,
To me, the poet stands
intently waiting
on the surface
of the deep totality, where it
crinkles into shape, sound
and object

and by writing there
and living there
becomes a compact
form of God

She does what God does
in some tiny way
and so shares the job
shares the life
and shares the level
where nothing spins
unless he spun it

it makes me
pause, at least
among the notes
and the steps
of the dance

just as your eyes
never blinking,
make me think that

though we're dancing
someone, something here
is unmoved, unmoving

unturned, unspun
not twirling, and
not turning sideways
in a languid, lovely fall

yet I, the master planner of your move
your turn, your twirl, your lift
have been the one

above the dance
uplifted

I touched a fly
today, on the wing

It was cleaning itself

My fingernail
moved the wing

and the fly

moved it back

But That's Nothing

The thing is that
Chip is still racing me down the big hill
By the Campus school
Where when we get to the bottom,
We hop off our bikes
And see how far they will go by themselves
Until they curl up and fall;

Diann is still rolling over in her cotton pyjamas
In her backyard, both of us wrapped in a blanket,
Me fully clothed, and while the night stars
Continue their timeless dance across the sky,
She looks down at my mouth,
Takes a soft little breath, and
Those perfect lips are slowly moving my way;

Dad is still ordering twenty seven
basketball players around the floor;

Arden is suspended in mid air,
As he jumps the tennis net, in the newsphoto
Just after winning the state high school tournament
Just before leaving for Denmark as an AFS student;

Richard is still in the middle of a jumpshot
Knees pulled up, seemingly six feet off the floor
In another win over Jesup High School;

Mom is laughing and mixing a batch of krumkake;

Mary is putting on makeup for South Pacific;

And Jan is smiling her first shy smile
That once caught the eye of Dan McNamara

But that's nothing,

Since also, Grant is coming over the riverbank
filled with worry, going into his first battle as a General,
and then, seeing that the Rebs had taken off,
realizes that they are as afraid of his men
as they of them, and loses that problem forever;

There's a click as Little Boy separates from Enola Gay
And is now two inches down in its fall
Toward wartime Hiroshima, while
Shizuo Izaki turns to the left
And has a last opinion about
the arrangement of flowers along the river;

Caesar steps out into the sunlight
On his way to the forum
On March 15;

And Basho hears a frog splashing
For the first time.

But that's nothing,

Because the origin of all languages
Is only inches away from where you are sitting,
Although to say inches is way too far away,
Since the entire history of creation is everywhere,
The past is omnipresent, as is the future
At least according to quantum physics
Where all the virtual events are constantly occurring

But not really occurring at the same time
And the whole idea that time is passing
Is just a convenience for the rest of us.

But that's nothing,

Since what that means is that
I'm still in love with you
Though it could be that we haven't met,
And we are already the perfect flow
Of the parts back to the whole,
We constantly pull the world back together
Just like the drops of water
Leap off the cliff at Niagara
And together, gather in a roar
As they fall, forever,
back toward the center

What the Moon Heard

The moon heard the wind
blowing through your heart

Saw the stream of
doubts, memories

Men falling by the way
eddying about
downwind

But then,
in what some other
unearthly body
might call silence

The moon heard
the thin, high
pure tone
of your love

Calling someone
home.

Diane Frank

I bought your poetry book
Yesterday, for ten dollars
For cripes sake
And, let's face it,
I thought that was overpricing it
For a poetry book.
I mean, they Xerox 'em up
And staple 'em together and
wham you owe ten bucks for poems,
and after all I've got 300 of the jokers
of my own, molding away in a whiskey box.
But, I thought, hey, think of it as subsidizing the arts
& so wrote the check and you went off happy
& I'm left with this
"Rhododendron Shedding its Skin"

And THEN (the nerve..)
it turns out that it's UNDERPRICED!
Not only is the binding perfect
And the paper wonderful
And warm with speckles
Like brown stars in a tan universe,
The book absolutely refuses to
Act like a book!

It's here right now on my nightstand
Looking innocent.
But when I open it
I end up in Egypt
On a Persian rug or
Listening to water in Brooklyn,

I meet several men
Watch you love them and
Leave them, with that special trick you have
Of letting them think they're leaving you
And then I get stuck out there on the edge
Where all of these unusual
But wonderfully important
Phrases fly by:

>The dream's
>Intersection with the world

>A dagger full of light

>Gestures of prairie

>Between the worlds
>A crack opens

>Below the membrane, the soul
>Comes floating in

And I'm left misquoting the Joker:
"Where does she get all those wonderful toys?"

And now the book
is bigger than my room by far
and I am afraid to open it
in case I might not get back.
And even now I'm worried
that I'm not really back
and never will be, again,
and not only that
that somehow you deserve

more money,
more happiness,
or pure consciousness
undifferentiated and yet palpable
as payment for the sight of
golden sparkle in everything I see,
even the inside of my eyelids

and that somehow
I owe you more for this.

And at the same time
I want more from you
Like knowing
How you catch those
Unusual words
Out in right field
On your delicate wing,
Those 'gifts of adobe,'
Many of them,
Circling now
Clamoring to get in
To the inky womb
Of your pen
for birth as something like (let me try):
Mendota boatways, or
delineations in rock, or
the unmarked path / of the butterfly,

or something on the broad back
of your last boyfriend forever
in the delicate, frozen silence
of sleep, lying in total innocence
while his soul floats in the stars

filled with love for you
filled with adoration
for you, Diana,
Goddess of the hunt,
Who found at last

The perfect man
The perfect phrase
The perfect key
To enter the silent space
Between the poetry, the love
The opinions and discussions

All held in place
By your hand on the wall
In the photo
On the back of your book
And in that silence, discover
What you knew all along
The space, the phrase, the key, the man, the love,
The Rhododendron Shedding It's Skin
It was Diana after all
The great one,
The big one,
The great Self,
The big huntress
Who when she places her
Sensitive hand
On the concrete wall
Sends trembles through
Every wall in Creation
Even all the ancient,
Dry, white and lost
Adobe.

Reach out
And touch this poem

Can you feel this poem

Reaching out
To touch you?

A Bullet Was Never Beautiful

No more
holding guns.
No holding guns in the hand.
No more long metal cylinders
with a hole at one end.
No more explosive charges
built to impel a metal bullet
down a long metal cylinder
with a hole
at one end.
No matter what those who love them say
a gun was never a beautiful thing.
There have been beautiful hands, beautiful bowls,
beautiful scarves,
But a gun was always meant to break or hurt something.
The only time gunpowder was beautiful was when it was
fireworks.
And that was a beautiful place to stop.
A bullet was never beautiful.
A bullet was never beautiful, intricate, intelligent,
interconnected
and delicate and tender and soft and surprising
like the inside of a human body is.
A bullet was never more beautiful than the body it invaded.
No more holding your hand still
so that the handle has something to push off from,
so that the barrel has something to maintain an aim,
so that the bullet must take on itself all of the momentum
and fly out at something/body/one.
No more aiming a gun at any one.
You can aim flowers, you can aim love,

but not a gun, ever again.
It's just not friendly, nice, or kind, and most of all,
not beautiful.
No more enemies.
No one has to be killed anymore.
They have to learn how to live.
And not just living like we have been living,
but fully alive, fully awake, fully in love,
conscious, enlightened living.
There are ways to become enlightened now. It's not just talk.
And it's not insignificant.
It's because of the general lack of enlightenment
that we still have general darkness and guns.
No more wargames.
No more video games where you kill or waste anyone or
anything.
No more fun shooting things or people up.
It's not that far in the mind
from shooting pixels to shooting people.
No more practicing to make things die.
Plant a seed.
Water a plant.
Enter the frictionless river of natural law
where even your thoughts will stop polluting.
Until that day
we are all the problem
we are all the limitation
we are all the reason
for the tears and pain.
Let go of anything that may move too quickly
at the living body of another
and be the beauty,
only beauty.

Eat light

(the angels do,

gathering at the dawn)

I Turn My Back

When I think
of the American Flag, today
it has changed to black,
white and gray
and it is flying upside down

In my dream, tonight
when the president's
motorcade passes
the crowd doesn't wave,
or cheer, or even watch.

Tomorrow, I write my
imaginary poem
in French,
in shame for
what's happening
in English,
and in honor of
what's been said
in France.

Right now, sitting alone,
just one American,
with no public
no voice, and
no microphone
I turn my back
on Washington
and look away

Je Tourne Mon Dos

Aujourdhui,
quand je pense
au drapeau
de mon pays,
il a tourné au gris
et blanc et noir,
et il vole au vent renversé

Dans mon rêve, ce soir,
quand la limousine
du président passe
devant les foules,
ce ne sont plus les gestes
d'accueil et de joie,
si pourtant on lève les yeux
pour le regarder. . .

Maintenant, j'ecris
en français,
honteux de ce
qui se passe
en anglais,
et en honneur
de ce qui a été dit
en France

Un Américain seul,
sans public,
sans voix,
sans microphone,
je tourne mon dos
à Washington
et regarde au loin

Notice
how the sound
emits
from the silent
left
margin.

Sometimes

Sometimes the purpose
of all civilization,
business,
education
and religion

Is just so a child can
sit in a field
of dandelions
alone and play.

family

Childhood Night

The clock downstairs
and its special chime
on the hour and quarter

The owl's hoot now and then
and the crumbs from
Grandma Stokstad's wheat germ
in the kitchen, silent.

The tiny football
hugged in in one arm,
and the fluorescent football outline
glowing on the chest
of my footed pyjamas,

Deep in the early years of the fifties,
Grandma still living, and
all of Stoughton, Wisconsin
fast asleep.

Richard

And when you turned to wave
You turned

And when you turned to wave
You waved

And when you turned to wave
I knew that you were going

The Eyes of a Poet

Little Ruthie, you stood so tall
in the wedding photo of a relative.

You stood and looked so very far
with eyes wide open, even at five.

You dominated the photo
of Norwegian American relatives.

Those eyes that now see God
in the arrival of a sparrow
at your breadcrumbs,

Those eyes of a mother
that look with forgiveness
where others see lack

Those eyes of a poet
that saw beyond, that see more

That gazed into the distance
and always will.

Grandfather, They Say You Read Thoreau

Grandfather,
Your painting of the stones and trees
Is darkened, damaged,
No one understands.
You live in photographs, paint-spattered,
Or in your Stoughton Restaurant,
Surrounded by your jars
The orange crush, the julep;
It is thirties, quaint,
Except for that it's yours
And you died my first year
Reaching for an envelope.

Independence Three

I. The Screen Inside

Paul
my little son
came
to the Independence
State Hospital
to see his mother
It broke his mother's heart
when he could
not be allowed
to be with her
He had to sit outside
a screen and talk
The tears fell from
his eyes
and I tried
to keep from showing
my feelings

—Ruth Stokstad

II. Outside the Screen

I don't remember crying
at all
I remember grey paint
and the long drive to Independence
and back.
I remember trying
to be strong for you
though I never understood
the separation.

III. The Screen Itself

They rest, these atoms
in shiny steel, and
though painted with the dullest
of institutional greys
they never know it.
They started in the earth
They went through the foundry
They were extruded into wire
and now this half century
they are a wire-mesh screen
in the door on Ward C.

That is, until
this door too is discarded,
left outside the building
or buried and returned
to rust, to dust
to pure mineral form, again,
only to come up as
iron in a plant
red color in the ground
or just part of the weightiness
that swings this world
round and round.

Yes it's true
that the screen itself
is changing
and that someday
in the space that divided
that which is you
from that which is me
there will be nothing
but an open
window.

In the Gym

The soft echo of rubber shoes
in the enormous cavern
of the dark gymnasium
Walking to a meeting, today,
alone across the basketball court.

The smell of netting and paint,
sweat and liniment,
The quiet of sounds that don't return,
the net in the hoop, torn and hanging,

and then, the thought of my father
a hundred and fifty-two miles away,
the old Coach, composing and rhyming,
typing and erasing,

Where once twenty strong young players
jumped to his order and call
with windsprints, layups,
halftime strategies, and plays
first scribbled on a paper napkin
at a Sunday restaurant.

Where once five year olds swam
clutching a blue board
to his open arms.

Where the stopwatch, the class list,
and the requisition filled his day.

Where tennis trophies piled up
in boxes in the garages of his students.

Now, grey-haired, he moves from
paper filled room to paper filled room
the Christian radio station on,
and writes rhymed inspirational verse.

Where is that Coach tonight?
Who hugged you after your big win,
who held your hand and showed you
how to shoot, the left hand under the ball
and the wrist flick of the right?

Where is that Coach
who sat through your entire
twelve and under tennis final
you in your pleated
Fred Perry tennis skirt, and
his kids in the car, waiting,

Where is that Coach, who gave you
the dropshot, the lob, the stop volley,
and said, over and over,
"Start through low, follow through high"

Where is he?

The old coach lives on,
typing into the night
in a little apartment in Des Moines.

For Mother

The rain pours off of the
metal corrugated roof
of the old barn
unexpectedly
and yet obvious:
in a hundred streams

The shiny blue bodied
bug crawling on the
light blue sheet
its torso flexible
unlike anything
I've ever seen

The sound and not the sight
of a crowd of birds
departing overhead

All this is so
that Ruthie will know
that all is well.

New Ache

There's a new
ache in my heart
like a balloon,
growing, pushing
trying to get out
and float free

and it's just because
of your baby hand
resting in mine,

your climb,
still a bit awkward
up onto the couch
only to sit on my lap
and have me read you
the book you brought

your head, finally
giving up to rest
on my shoulder
as I bounce you
hoping for sleep
to the Norah
Jones album
again

it's your tiny bite
from my sandwich

your shriek of delight
while galloping around
the living room

your every tear
for hitting your head
for mommy leaving
for being up too late
(I dream of saving
every one)

There is no gold
to outweigh or value
this feeling

as you lean over
in your high chair
to give me a little
broken piece
of your
avocado

and friends

Nancy's Hand

Nancy's hand rests on my table,
in between small, explanatory flights
around the room

I hear her talking, and respond
but my heart, jealous, stares
at her little hand

While my eyes tear up
at the hand that gets to be
with Nancy Berg every day

The hand that gets to be in L.A.
with Nancy all the time

The hand that serves her
with writing, cleaning, holding a pencil,
and playing with her hair

That hand, like a kid
in a wealthy family
who makes the rest of us
want to be so lucky, if only
for a day or two

Still, now I take her hand, in my mind
and make it a secret ally
so that when I can't be there
to have fun with her
and go glittering through
Nancy days and nights

Her hand can be there for me
to help her, to be attached to her
and to admire her
at arms length, forever.

Don't Worry, Be Happy

Don't fall down while you're jogging
And lie unconscious
To be taken by an ambulance
And wake up in the hospital
And miss work.

Don't worry about things
And feel unable to get it straight.

Don't let love or not love get to you
You have lots of love to give,
Ask your Mountain kitty

Don't ever get sick or be unhappy or
Up and die on me.

I feel responsible on some level
To protect you, to keep you happy.

Don't ever feel alone in all the world
Or in despair, or forgotten,
You are never forgotten.

Don't ever worry "will I ever have children?"
Your drawings are children,
You comfort people, who feel, childlike,

And if we never had one
I want to tell you that I wish we had
So we could have crossed that threshold
Just like we left the doorway
Of Elim Lutheran Church,
Young, fresh, uniformed, but brave.

Don't worry about anything.
Be happy.

The world has love,
And I send it to you.

Dancing in Paradise Café

I'm on the floor
with my foot extended to Cassiopeia,
toe pointing to the Pole Star.
I'm twirling into the birth
of a new galaxy,
swirling gasses condensing into the shape
of the choreography of your
left arm
as you pull me into
the salty water of a lunar sea,
where life, against all odds,
is finding its first form,
molecules colliding into cells
discovering the prelude to the sonata
of first light.

It's a dinosaur's dream,
the edge of a bone,
the heartbeat of a feather
finding the species and genus
of a bird that will fly
into the dance of fingers
exploring the shape of a star
at the apogee
of a dream inside of an egg
etched with the wisdom
of an exploding universe.

It's the chanting of an ocean,
as it discovers the shape
of a heartbeat

Dancing in Paradise Café

He's sitting
left arm over the back
of the booth in the bookstore
that has seen
many a lunch
framed in
paperback dreams
I haven't met him yet
But will, soon, and
Even now, I'm happy
Seeing him, feet extended
Out into the walkway
Laptop on the gnarled
Wood table, part of what
Makes this place beautiful

It's amazing, like a dream,
To walk out of Café Paradiso
And then in passing the next
Intersection northward
To simply see Diane,
Walking through,
And then to walk and talk
Excitedly with her
And of course to discover
That the love she is meeting
I have already seen, already admired

I'm as if chanting
What I have said so many times
You support her this way

and remembers how to dance,
light inside the
breath of the buffalo
running across a primal plain
of first light,
writing on the wall of the cave
where the ocean echoes,
a forest of aspens dancing,
back arcing into the curve
of the penumbra of a silver moon.

And the flute's high descant vibrato
singing the memory of the future
where the secret of species is revealed
in the chord of the whir of grasshoppers
on a blue and emerald jewel
in the shape of a double helix,
remembering the white fire
in the belt of Orion,
an arrow through time
dreaming the beauty of the Pleiades,
the temple dancer,
her silver bells, her back
a sequences of vectors
across oceans, across time.

Diane Frank

You don't really bend
You let her be the curve
While you are the tall line
You bring her close to you
And stay in your strength
As I show him, right there
How to do the death drop
How to do the arabesque lift
And all of the secret leads
That let her know what's next

And then she like a slender flute
Sways and lifts,
Even so, he wonders
Can I really lift all that?
And, man to man
We talk, of how to deal
With such a beauty
Such a dreamer, even
When she is at her lowest
And how we never even try
To lift her, but only lean
In the right direction
And then she flows, with us
Into the new.

Paul Stokstad

Tennis

To some people
Tennis is a sort of minor sport
On TV, with hushed commentary
Heads turning, back and forth

But to me
Its summers spent,
Dragging the broad broom
over the green clay
and then sweeping the lines
For the afternoon players

It's the future homecoming queen
Still only twelve years old
Already impossibly lovely
In her pleated skirt, gliding left
To hit her underspin shot
Deep to the corner

It's my hair, bleaching from brown
To blond, from day after day
Spent on the court

It's standing frozen, breathless
In front of the 1957 Playboy shot
of Marilyn Monroe
On the inside wall
of Norris' broom shed

It's picking up
Thousands of balls
After my Father's group lessons

And the thought that
He may still see me now
out there

Playing his game.

Butterfly Tattoo

Right now it's Mardi Gras outside my window
and the biggest part of the parade has passed
but I can still see, smell, and taste
crawfish étouffe, someone making a roux
and the float with the gorgeous,
22-foot high libra nude
with her magical breasts still growing
and the balloons with all of our insights
and philosophical and spiritual experiences
written all over them,
and the time we kissed in the forest
in the cold fall wind, after a year apart,

And now the giant clown comes floating by
over the roof, late, grinning and waving, unshaven,
and there, on the corner, still drinking, smoking
and swaggering in leather jackets
all the stuff we used to fight about

And just beyond them
in a pure white and golden mist
with sparkles only visible
in a higher state of consciousness
the simple love that I followed,
straight through the thugs
every time we got back together

Yes, it's Mardi Gras
and though I don't ever get drunk
I did get distracted
and just now I woke up
alone, again,
with the thought of
your butterfly tattoo
flying, leaving, gone,
but under my skin
forever.

About the Author

For the first few decades, Paul was mostly interested in girls, tennis and pole vaulting. In college he dabbled in theatre, wearing long hair and an earring, and did some poetry writing at the U of Iowa undergraduate writers workshop, receiving a "Citation for Excellence in Creative Writing." Later interests have included ad copywriting, disco, improv theatre, attachment parenting, and Netflix. He self-published a tennis book and an improv theater book. The latter is ranked 2,171,018 on Amazon. He has been practicing Transcendental Meditation twice a day since 1970, though he did miss once in 1997 (he still blames Deborah). He has a BA in English, an MA in English and Linguistics, an MA in the Science of Creative Intelligence, and some kind of honorary Ph.D in World peace, from MERU, we think. Professionally he has worked mostly in advertising and web marketing, and as of May 2012 serves as the Marketing Director for MUM.edu.

www.ingramcontent.com/pod-product-compliance
Lightning Source LLC
Chambersburg PA
CBHW020942100426
42741CB00006BA/616